*For Ff ★ D.M.*

Text by Lois Rock
Illustrations copyright © 2003 Diana Mayo
This edition copyright © 2003 Lion Publishing

The moral rights of the author and illustrator
have been asserted

Published by
**Lion Publishing plc**
Mayfield House, 256 Banbury Road,
Oxford OX2 7DH, England
www.lion-publishing.co.uk
ISBN 0 7459 4794 8

First edition 2003
1 3 5 7 9 10 8 6 4 2 0

**Acknowledgments**
Scripture quotations on pp. 6, 9, 16 and 20
quoted from the Good News Bible published by
The Bible Societies/HarperCollins Publishers Ltd, UK
© American Bible Society 1966, 1971, 1976, 1992,
used with permission.

A catalogue record for this book is available
from the British Library

Typeset in 13/18 Garamond ITC Lt BT
Printed and bound in Singapore

# The
# *Christmas Story*

**Retold by Lois Rock**
*from the Gospels of Matthew and Luke*

**Illustrated by Diana Mayo**

LION
Children's Books

The little town of Nazareth lies among the hills of Galilee. Long ago, it was the home of a young woman named Mary. She was looking forward to getting married. Her husband-to-be, Joseph, could trace his family back hundreds of years to the people's greatest king, David.

One day, God sent the angel Gabriel to visit Mary.

'Peace be with you!' said the angel. 'The Lord is with you and has greatly blessed you!'

Mary was alarmed. Who was this visitor? What did the words mean?

'Don't be afraid,' said the angel. 'God has been good to you. You will become pregnant, and you will have a son. You are to call him Jesus, and God will make him a king, like King David of old.'

'How can this be?' asked Mary. 'I am not yet married!'

The angel explained that the child would be
God's: Jesus would be God's own Son.
'I will do as God wants,' agreed Mary.

Mary soon found out that the angel's words were coming true: she was pregnant. She went to visit her cousin Elizabeth. Elizabeth was much older than Mary. She had never had any children, and everyone had thought she was now too old; but then came the surprise news that she was expecting a baby. Mary wanted to tell her news to Elizabeth first of all.

As soon as Mary entered the house, Elizabeth felt her own baby jump inside her for joy, and by the power of God she understood at once what was happening to Mary.

'You are the most blessed of all women, and blessed is the child you will bear!' she exclaimed.

Mary sang a joyful song to God:

'My heart praises God,
and my soul is glad:
for God has remembered me;
and from now on everyone
will say that I am blessed.
God has done great things for me;
God will do great things for us:
for God is on the side of those who are poor;
God helps those who have no one else to
    defend them.
God will bless our people, as promised so
    long ago.
God will bless us all.'

Mary stayed with Elizabeth for three months. When she went back to Nazareth, there was important news: the emperor in Rome wanted to know how many people there were in his empire, so he could order them to pay taxes. Everyone had to go and register their names in their home town.

Joseph's home town was Bethlehem – the place where King David had been born. As his wife-to-be, Mary had to go with him.

Together they made the long journey south, into the region of Judea. When they arrived, they found that the town was bustling with

travellers. There was no room left anywhere.

Mary desperately needed somewhere to stay, for her baby was soon to be born.

At last Mary and Joseph found shelter in a place that was normally kept for animals. There, Mary had her baby.

She swaddled him snugly in strips of cloth. Now all she needed was to find a cradle.

There was a manger in the room. It was only a feeding trough for the animals, but it was sturdy and dry. Mary's little baby could sleep there and be safe.

The little family lay down to rest as the stars shone in the night sky.

Out on the hillsides that sloped down from the town, the shepherds had little chance to sleep. They had to stay out in the fields, making sure that their flocks were safe from wild animals and thieves. The night was quiet and still, but they were always on the alert.

Suddenly, one of God's angels appeared, and the glory of heaven shone all around. The shepherds were very afraid.

'Don't be afraid,' said the angel. 'I bring good news. This very day in David's town a baby has been born. He is the Christ, God's chosen king, the one who will save you and all your people.

'Here is a sign, to prove to you that my words are true. You will find a baby wrapped in strips of cloth and lying in a manger.'

T hen a great crowd of angels appeared, praising God and singing: 'Glory to God in the highest heaven, and peace on earth to those with whom God is pleased!'

The angels went away, and the shepherds looked at one another in amazement.

'Then let's go to Bethlehem,' they said.
So they went and found Mary, Joseph and the
baby. Everything was just as the angels had said.

Joseph looked down at Mary's little baby. He remembered the time, months earlier, just after he had found out that Mary was pregnant. How upset he had been, how ashamed. The baby was not his, he knew that. He had wanted to break off the engagement and leave Mary to sort out her own future.

Then, in a dream, an angel had spoken to him: 'Joseph, do not be afraid to marry Mary; for her child is God's own Son. You are to call him Jesus, because he will save his people from all the wrong that they do.'

Now Joseph smiled at the child. 'I name you Jesus,' he said proudly.

19

Meanwhile, far away, men who studied the stars had seen something special: a new star in the eastern sky, a sign that a new king had been born.

They came to the city of Jerusalem asking, 'Where is the baby born to be the king of the Jews? We saw his star when it came up in the east, and we have come to worship him.'

But there was already a king of the Jews in Jerusalem: King Herod. He ruled the country on behalf of the emperor and was famous for his cruelty towards anyone who threatened his power.

He was alarmed and summoned the priests and learned advisers.

'Tell me more about the promise God made to send a king to rescue the people,' he said, 'the promise of a Messiah, a Christ. Where will he be born?'

'In Bethlehem,' they answered. 'So it is written in our scriptures.'

Herod smiled grimly as he took in the news, and then he barked an order to his servants: 'Fetch the travellers that everyone is talking about.'

At a secret meeting, Herod asked many questions about the star – when it had appeared and what it meant. Then he sent the men to Bethlehem. 'Go and find the king,' he said, 'and when you do, come and let me know, so I may go and worship him too.'

The travellers left. On their way, the star they had seen in the east shone ahead of them. It stopped right over the place where the child was.

The men went inside, and there they found the child, Jesus, with his mother, Mary. They knelt to worship him. They brought out their gifts of gold, frankincense and myrrh, and gave them to the child.

That night, as they rested before beginning the journey home, they had a dream. God warned them not to go back to Herod. The next day, they set out for home by a different route.

An angel also came and spoke to Joseph in a dream. 'Beware,' said the angel, 'Herod will be looking for the child and will want to kill him. Hurry! Take your family far away to where they will be safe.'

So, in the night, Mary, Joseph and Jesus fled from Bethlehem.

Later, when the time was right, the little family returned to Nazareth in Galilee. There, Jesus grew and became strong. He was full of wisdom, and God's blessings were upon him.